MY FIRST JOKES AND RIDDLES

Waiter, Do You Serve Lobster?

by Judy Ziegler

GALLERY BOOKS

An Imprint of W. H. Smith Publishers Inc.
112 Madison Avenue
New York City 10016

An RGA Book

Why did the walrus grease the monkey?

He wanted to see a monkey shine.

How did the mouse talk to the elephant?

He used big words.

Where do traveling groundhogs live?

What do you call a six-pack of soda?

A pop group.

What did the big rose say to the little rose?

"Hi, bud!"

How do you make your pants last?

Why do dragons make bad bosses?

They fire everyone.

What side of a house do elm trees grow on?

The outside.

What did the snake say to the dentist?

"Fangs a lot!"

Why did the alligator take his clock to the bank?

He wanted to save time.

Why couldn't the butterfly go to the dance?

It was a moth ball.

What do bullfrogs drink?

Croak-a-cola.

"Waiter, do you have frog legs?"

"No, I just walk this way."

What do you call a bad-tempered buffalo
wearing earplugs?

Anything you want. He can't hear you.

What word do antelopes always spell w-r-o-n-g?

Wrong.

What do you do if your dog chews up your book?

Take the words right out of his mouth.

What kind of dog has no tail?

A corn dog.

What can a wombat hold in his right paw but not his left?

His left elbow.

What do slugs drink?

What's a rabbit's favorite song?

Hoppy Birthday.